T5-AGD-184

VOICES of FREEDOM

English for U.S. Government and Citizenship

Book 1

Bill Bliss

with
Steven J. Molinsky

PRENTICE HALL REGENTS
Englewood Cliffs, New Jersey 07632

Library of Congress Cataloging-in-Publication Data
Bliss, Bill.
    Voices of freedom/Bill Bliss, with Steven J. Molinsky.

        p. cm.
    Contents: 1. English for United States Government and Citizenship.
    ISBN   0-13-944026-7 (v.1)
    1. United States—Politics and Government.   2. United States—History.
    I. Molinsky, Steven J.   II. Title.
    JK 1758.B59   1989
    320.473—dc19   89-3565
                                                                        CIP

Editorial/production supervision and
  interior design: Janet Johnston
Cover design: Sue Paxman
Manufacturing buyer: Sheila Meyer
Project photographer: Paul I. Tanedo
Spanish translation: Rebecca Robles and Michael Zamba

The cooperation of students and staff of the
Arlington Education and Employment Program
and the INS Legalization Office in Arlington, Virginia
is gratefully acknowledged.

© 1989 by Prentice-Hall, Inc.
A Division of Simon & Schuster
Englewood Cliffs, New Jersey 07632

All rights reserved. No part of this book may be
reproduced, in any form or by any means,
without permission in writing from the publisher.

Printed in the United States of America

10   9   8   7   6   5   4   3   2

ISBN 0-13-944026-7

Prentice-Hall International (UK) Limited, *London*
Prentice-Hall of Australia Pty. Limited, *Sydney*
Prentice-Hall Canada, Inc., *Toronto*
Prentice-Hall Hispanoamericana, S.A., *Mexico*
Prentice-Hall of India Private Limited, *New Delhi*
Prentice-Hall of Japan, Inc., *Tokyo*
Prentice-Hall of Southeast Asia Pte. Ltd., *Singapore*
Editora Prentice-Hall do Brasil, Ltda., *Rio de Janeiro*

Dedicated to Benjamin and Flora Bliss, Nathan and
Sophia Bliss, and Nat and Betty Meister.

Photo Credits:
Page **2,4,6,10,12,18,20,22,24,26,36,40,66,72,80** by Paul I.
Tanedo.

Page **38** A.T.&T. Photo Center; **46** Irene Springer; **49** *top*
Larry Fleming; *bottom left* Irene Springer; *bottom right*
Stan Wakefield; **52** *top left* Marc Anderson; *top right*
NASA; *bottom right* Larry Fleming; **54** *left and middle*
Marc Anderson; *right* Stan Wakefield; **56** *top and middle*
Courtesy of United Airlines; *bottom* Irene Springer; **58**
UPI/Bettmann Newsphotos; **59** *left* AP/Wide World
Photos; *right* UPI/Bettmann Newsphotos; **64** United
Airlines; **67** *left* AP/Wide World Photos; *right* UPI/
Bettmann Newsphotos; **69** UPI/Bettmann Newsphotos; **76**
Irene Springer; **78** *left* John Spragens, Jr.; **81** *left* Arvind
Garg; *middle* Arthur Glauberman; *right* Carl Scholfield;
82 National Archives; **83** Library of Congress.

Cover photo: Daniel Carver

CONTENTS

TO THE STUDENT

Good luck as you study English, history, and government, and good luck in your interview at the I.N.S.

I wish you a happy and healthy life here in your new country.

Welcome to the United States of America!

Bill Bliss
Washington, D.C.

PERSONAL INFORMATION
IDENTIFICATION CARDS
FORM I-698 (APPLICATION TO ADJUST
STATUS FROM TEMPORARY TO
PERMANENT RESIDENT)
NUMBERS & ALPHABET

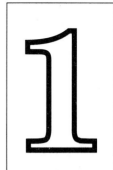

Temporary Resident
Temporary Resident Card
Could You Spell That, Please?
Numbers
My Address
What's Your File Number?

Functional Interview Skills

Reporting Personal Information
Asking for Clarification

Grammar

To Be
WH-Questions
Numbers
Alphabet

Related Practice

ExpressWays Foundations: Chapter 1
ExpressWays Book One: Chapter 1
Side by Side Second Edition Book 1: Chapters 1, 2, 3
Side by Side First Edition Book 1A: Chapters 1, 2, 3

Temporary Resident

My name is Carlos Rivera.
My first name is Carlos.
My last name is Rivera.

I'm a temporary resident.
I'm applying for amnesty.
I'm applying for permanent residence.

CHECK-UP

Circle the Same Word

1. name	first	(name)	last
2. My	I'm	is	My
3. last	last	amnesty	first
4. amnesty	name	first	amnesty
5. first	amnesty	last	first
6. temporary	permanent	temporary	residence

Vocabulary Check

temporary	applying	last	amnesty	name

1. My ___*name*___ is Carlos Rivera.

2. I'm applying for _____.

3. My _____ name is Rivera.

4. I'm a _____ resident.

5. I'm _____ for permanent residence.

How About You?

1. What's your first name? _____

2. What's your last name? _____

Temporary Resident Card

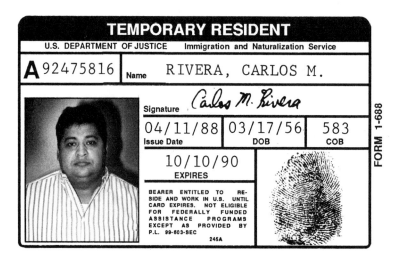

I'm a temporary resident.
This is my temporary resident card.

My family name* is Rivera.
My first name is Carlos.
My middle name is Manuel.
My full name is Carlos Manuel Rivera.

I'm applying for amnesty.
I'm applying for permanent residence.

*family name = last name
            surname

CHECK-UP

Grammar Check

a	from	My	I'm	is

1. My first name _____ is _____ Carlos.

2. _____ middle name is Manuel.

3. I'm _____ temporary resident.

4. _____ applying for permanent residence.

5. I'm _____ Mexico.

What's Your Name?

1. _____ _____ _____
   First Name   Middle Name   Last Name

2. _____ _____ _____
   Last Name   First Name   Middle Name

3. _____
   (Family Name) (First Name) (Middle Name)

4. □□□□□□□□□□□ □□□□□□□□□□□ □□□□□□□□□
   Family Name   First   Middle

Fill Out the Form

Example

Family Name *(Last Name in CAPITAL Letters) (See instructions) (First Name) (Middle Name)*
RIVERA Carlos Manuel

1.
Family Name *(Last Name in CAPITAL Letters) (See instructions) (First Name) (Middle Name)*

2.
Family Name *(Last Name in CAPITAL Letters) (See instructions) (First Name) (Middle Name)*

INTERVIEW

Could You Spell That, Please?

The Alphabet
Aa Bb Cc Dd Ee Ff Gg Hh Ii Jj Kk Ll Mm
Nn Oo Pp Qq Rr Ss Tt Uu Vv Ww Xx Yy Zz

A. What's your family name?

B. Rivera.

A. Could you spell that, please?

B. R-I-V-E-R-A.

A. What's your first name?

B. Carlos.

A. And your middle name?

B. Manuel.

A. What's your family name?

B. _____.

A. Could you spell that, please?

B. _____.

A. What's your first name?

B. _____.

A. And your middle name?

B. _____.*

Practice with another student, using the model dialog above as a guide. Take turns being the INS examiner and the applicant.

*If no middle name, say "I don't have a middle name."

6

CHECK-UP

Alphabet Practice

Fill in the missing letters of the alphabet. Then use the letters to make a word.

1. Ⓐ B C D Ⓔ F G H I J K L Ⓜ Ⓝ O P Q R S T U V W X Y Z

   Ⓝ Ⓐ Ⓜ Ⓔ

2. ☐ B ☐ ☐ E F G H I J K L M N O P Q ☐ S T U V W X Y Z

   ☐ ☐ ☐ ☐

3. ☐ B C D E F G H I J K ☐ M N O P Q R ☐ ☐ U V W X Y Z

   ☐ ☐ ☐ ☐

4. ☐ B C D ☐ F G H I J K L ☐ ☐ O P Q R ☐ ☐ U V W X ☐ Z

   ☐ ☐ ☐ ☐ ☐ ☐

Listening

Listen and circle the correct answer.

1. (Martinez)   Rivera

2. Sanchez   Santos

3. Tran   Dang

4. Cruz   Ortiz

5. Long   Wong

Listen and write the name you hear.

1. Garcia _____   4. _____

2. _____   5. _____

3. _____   6. _____

Numbers

0	1	2	3	4	5	6	7	8	9

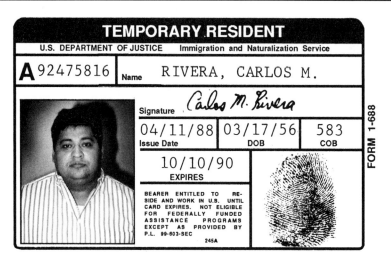

This is my temporary resident card.

My alien registration number is A-92475816.

This is my social security card.

My social security number is 408-37-1692.*

> **RIVERA Carlos M** 80 Stanley Av
> Los Angeles...................**257-9108**

This is my telephone number.

My telephone number is 257-9108.

*0 = "oh."

Check-Up

Matching

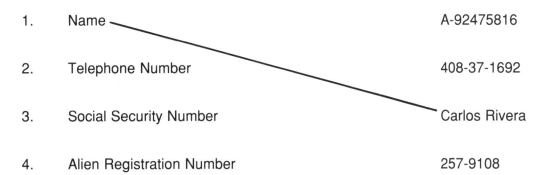

1. Name
2. Telephone Number
3. Social Security Number
4. Alien Registration Number

A-92475816

408-37-1692

Carlos Rivera

257-9108

Answer These Questions

1. What's your alien registration number?   A - _ _ _ _ _ _ _ _

2. What's your social security number?   _ _ _ - _ _ - _ _ _ _

3. What's your telephone number?   _ _ _ - _ _ _ _

4. What's your area code?   _ _ _

5. What's your home telephone number?   (_ _ _) _ _ _ - _ _ _ _
    (Include area code.)

6. What's your phone number at work?   (_ _ _) _ _ _ - _ _ _ _
    (Include area code.)

Fill Out the Form

Applicant's File No.
A. - 9 _ _ _ _ _ _ _
Family Name *(Last Name in CAPITAL Letters) (See instructions) (First Name) (Middle Name)*
Phone No.'s (Include Area Codes) Home: Work:
Enter your Social Security Number _ _ _ - _ _ - _ _ _ _

My Address

10	11	12	13	14	15	16	17	18	19

20	30	40	50	60	70	80	90

My address is 80 Stanley Avenue.
My apartment number is 12-D.
The name of my city is Los Angeles.
The name of my state is California.
Los Angeles is in California.
California is in the United States of America.
My zip code is 90048.

I'm applying for amnesty.
I'm applying for permanent residence in the
United States of America.

CHECK-UP

Matching

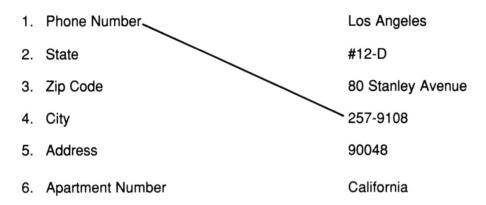

1. Phone Number   Los Angeles

2. State   #12-D

3. Zip Code   80 Stanley Avenue

4. City   257-9108

5. Address   90048

6. Apartment Number   California

Reading Addresses

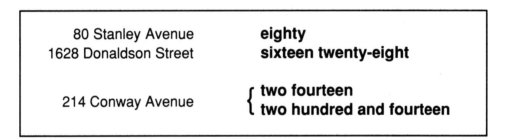

80 Stanley Avenue	**eighty**
1628 Donaldson Street	**sixteen twenty-eight**
214 Conway Avenue	{ **two fourteen** { **two hundred and fourteen**

Say these addresses.

13 Stanley Avenue   4826 Greenwood Avenue

60 Spring Street   594 Parkman Avenue

1360 Donaldson Street   842 Main Street

Listening

Listen and circle the number you hear.

1. 60   (30)   4. 4256   4615

2. 13   19   5. 1839   3918

3. 15   50   6. 482   842

INTERVIEW
What's Your File Number?

A. What's your file number?

B. You mean my alien registration number?

A. Yes.

B. It's A-92475816.

A. And what's your home telephone number? Area code first.

B. 213-257-9108.

A. And your work phone?*

B. 213-626-4377.

A. What's the name of your state?

B. California.

A. And your city?

B. Los Angeles.

A. What's your address?

B. 80 Stanley Avenue.

A. Apartment number?

B. 12-D.

A. Zip code?

B. 90048.

 * work phone = phone number at work

A. What's your file number?

B. You mean my alien registration number?

A. Yes.

B. It's A-_____.

A. And what's your home telephone number? Area code first.

B. _____.

A. And your work phone?

B. _____.

A. What's the name of your state?

B. _____.

A. And your city?

B. _____.

A. What's your address?

B. _____.

A. Apartment number?

B. _____.*

A. Zip code?

B. _____.

Practice with another student, using the model dialog above as a guide. Take turns being the INS examiner and the applicant.

* If no apartment number, say "No."

CHECK-UP

Write Your Home Address

1. Home Address: _____

   Number   Street   Apt. No.

   _____

   City   State   Zip Code

2. Home Address: ☐☐☐☐☐☐☐☐☐☐☐☐☐☐☐☐☐☐☐☐☐☐☐☐☐☐☐☐☐☐☐☐☐☐

   Number   Street   Apt. No.

   ☐☐☐☐☐☐☐☐☐☐☐☐☐☐☐☐☐☐☐☐☐☐☐☐☐   ☐☐☐   ☐☐☐☐☐

   City   State   Zip Code

3.
Home Address *(No. and Street)*	*(Apt No.)*	*(City)*	*(State)*	*(Zip Code)*

Fill Out the Form

Applicant's File No. A - 9 _ _ _ _ _ _ _	
Family Name *(Last Name in CAPITAL Letters)(See instructions) (First Name) (Middle Name)*	
Home Address *(No. and Street)* *(Apt No.)* *(City)* *(State)* *(Zip Code)*	
Phone No.'s *(Include Area Codes)* Home: Work:	Enter your Social Security Number _ _ _ . _ _ . _ _ _ _

DICTATION

Listen and write.

1. _____

2. _____

14

CHOICES

Choose the best answer.

       Example   My name is
                     A.   14-C.
                     B.   407-32-1289.
                     (C.) Hector Garcia.
                     D.   10023.

1. My alien registration number is
   A. 75215.
   B. 237-1264.
   C. A-95314728.
   D. 407-32-1289.

2. My social security number is
   A. 75215.
   B. 237-1264.
   C. A-95314728.
   D. 407-32-1289.

3. My home telephone number is
   A. 75215.
   B. 237-1264.
   C. A-95314728.
   D. 407-32-1289.

4. My zip code is
   A. 75215.
   B. 237-1264.
   C. A-95314728.
   D. 407-32-1289.

5. I'm a temporary
   A. amnesty.
   B. card.
   C. number.
   D. resident.

6. The name of my state is
   A. Los Angeles.
   B. California.
   C. the United States of America.
   D. Carlos Rivera.

REVIEW

Information Exchange

Read these questions and answer them.

What's your family name?
(Could you spell that, please?)
What's your first name?
What's your middle name?
What's your alien registration number?
What's your social security number?
What's your home address?
What's your apartment number?
What's the name of your city?
What's the name of your state?
What's your zip code?
What's your home telephone number? Area code first.
What's your work phone?

Now interview other students, using these questions. Write the information below.

1.

Applicant's File No.

A - 9 _ _ _ _ _ _ _

Family Name *(Last Name in CAPITAL Letters)(See instructions) (First Name) (Middle Name)*

Home Address *(No. and Street)*   *(Apt No.)*   *(City)*   *(State)*   *(Zip Code)*

Phone No.'s *(Include Area Codes)*
Home:
Work:

Enter your Social Security Number

_ _ _ - _ _ - _ _ _ _

2.

Applicant's File No.

A- 9 _ _ _ _ _ _ _

Family Name *(Last Name in CAPITAL Letters)(See instructions) (First Name) (Middle Name)*

Home Address *(No. and Street)*   *(Apt No.)*   *(City)*   *(State)*   *(Zip Code)*

Phone No.'s *(Include Area Codes)*
Home:
Work:

Enter your Social Security Number

_ _ _ - _ _ - _ _ _ _

PERSONAL INFORMATION
FORM I-698 (APPLICATION TO ADJUST
    STATUS FROM TEMPORARY TO
    PERMANENT RESIDENT)
MONTHS OF THE YEAR
DATES

I Was Born in Monterrey
What's Your Place of Birth?
What's Your Date of Birth?
Are You Still Living at 86 Central Avenue?
Let Me Verify Some Information

Functional Interview Skills

Reporting Personal Information
Asking for Clarification
Checking and Indicating Understanding
Responding to INS Examiner's Verification
of Form I-698 Information
Correcting

Grammar

To Be
WH-Questions
Yes/No Questions
Short Answers

Related Practice

ExpressWays Foundations: Chapter 2
ExpressWays Book One: Chapter 2
Side by Side Second Edition Book 1: Chapters 4, 5, 6
Side by Side First Edition Book 1A: Chapters 4, 5, 6

I Was Born in Monterrey

My name is Maria Lopez.
I'm from Mexico.
Now I'm in the United States of America.
The name of my city is Houston.
Houston is in the state of Texas.
Texas is a state in the United States.

I'm Mexican.
I was born in Monterrey.
Monterrey is in the state of Nuevo León.
Nuevo León is a state in Mexico.

I was born on May 4, 1962.
My mother's name is Gloria.
My father's name is Oscar.
My mother and father are in Monterrey.
I'm not in Monterrey.
I'm in Houston.
I'm applying for permanent residence in the
     United States of America.

CHECK-UP

Matching

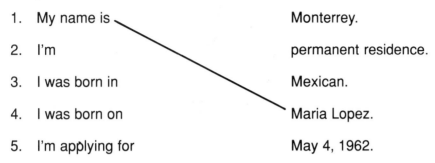

1. My name is   Monterrey.

2. I'm   permanent residence.

3. I was born in   Mexican.

4. I was born on   Maria Lopez.

5. I'm applying for   May 4, 1962.

Vocabulary Check

city	applying	born	name	mother	state

1. My ____*name*____ is Maria Lopez.

2. The name of my _____ is Houston.

3. The name of my _____ is Texas.

4. I was _____ in Monterrey.

5. My father and _____ are in Monterrey.

6. I'm _____ for permanent residence in the United States.

Fill Out the Form

Date of Birth

May 4, 1962 = 5/4/62
October 21, 1958 = 10/21/58

Family Name *(Last Name in CAPITAL Letters)(See instructions)* *(First Name) (Middle Name)*
Date of Birth *(Month/Day/Year)*

INTERVIEW
What's Your Place of Birth?

A. What's your place of birth?

B. Excuse me?

A. Where were you born? What's your native country?

B. I was born in Mexico.

A. In what city or town?

B. I was born in Monterrey.

A. Where is that?

B. Monterrey is in the state of Nuevo León.

A. What's your place of birth?

B. Excuse me?

A. Where were you born? What's your native country?

B. I was born in _____.

A. In what city or town?

B. I was born in _____.

A. Where is that?

B. _____ is in _____.

Practice with another student, using the model dialog above as a guide. Take turns being the INS examiner and the applicant.

CHECK-UP

Questions and Answers

Practice the different ways to ask these questions.

What's your nationality?	I'm **Mexican**.
What's your place of birth? What's your native country? What country are you from? Where were you born? Where are you from? }	**Mexico**.
In what city or town were you born? What city or town were you born in? Where were you born? }	I was born **in Monterrey**.

Now answer these questions.

1. What's your nationality? _____

2. What country are you from? _____

3. In what city or town were you born? _____

Grammar Check

Where	**What**

1. __What_____ is your nationality?

2. _____ were you born?

3. _____ country are you from?

4. _____ city or town were you born in?

5. _____ are you from?

What's Your Date of Birth?

A. What's your date of birth?

B. I'm sorry. I didn't understand. Could you please say that again?

A. When were you born?

B. I was born on May 4, 1962.

A. On May 4, 1962?

B. Yes. That's right.

A. And what's your mother's first name?

B. Gloria.

A. And your father's?

B. Oscar.

A. What's your date of birth?

B. I'm sorry. I didn't understand. Could you please say that again?

A. When were you born?

B. I was born on _____.

A. On _____?

B. Yes. That's right.

A. And what's your mother's first name?

B. _____.

A. And your father's?

B. _____.

Practice with another student, using the model dialog above as a guide. Take turns being the INS examiner and the applicant.

CHECK-UP

Months and Years

Practice the months of the year.

January	April	July	October
February	May	August	November
March	June	September	December

Practice reading the years.

1962	nineteen sixty-two
1957	nineteen fifty-seven
1776	seventeen seventy-six

Questions and Answers

Practice the different ways to ask these questions.

What year were you born?   }   I was born in **1962**.
In what year were you born?

In what month were you born?   I was born in **May**.

What's your date of birth?
What's your birth date?   }   I was born on **May 4, 1962**.
When were you born?

Now answer these questions.

1. What year were you born? _____

2. In what month were you born? _____

3. What's your date of birth? _____

INTERVIEW
Are You Still Living at 86 Central Avenue?

A. Are you still living at 86 Central Avenue?

B. Yes, I am.

A. And is your zip code 10715?

B. Yes, it is.

A. Are you still living at 65 Main Street?

B. No, I'm not.

A. 65 Main Street isn't your current address?

B. No, it isn't. My new address is 1247 Washington Street in Arlington.

A. And what's the zip code?

B. 22215.

A. Are you still living at _____?

B. Yes, I am.

A. And is your zip code _____?

B. Yes, it is.

A. Are you still living at _____?

B. No, I'm not.

A. _____ isn't your current address?

B. No, it isn't. My new address is _____

   in _____.

A. And what's the zip code?

B. _____.

Choose the dialog that fits your situation and practice with another student. Take turns being the INS examiner and the applicant.

CHECK-UP

Grammar Check

I am	I'm not	it is	it isn't

1. Are you still living at
   45 Park Street?

   Yes, __I am__ .

2. Is your zip code 10019?

   Yes, _____.

3. Are you from Guatemala?

   No, _____.

4. Is 1896 Central Avenue
   your current address?

   No, _____.

INTERVIEW
Let Me Verify Some Information

A. Let me verify some information on your I-698 form.* Your family name is Garcia. Is that right?

B. Yes, it is.

A. And your first name is Victor. Is that correct?

B. No, it isn't. My first name is Francisco. My MIDDLE name is Victor.

A. I see. Your nationality is Mexican?

B. Yes. That's right.

A. Born in Guadalajara?

B. Yes. That's correct.

A. And is your date of birth November 20, 1958?

B. No. That's not correct. My date of birth is OCTOBER 20, 1958.

A. All right. And what's your social security number?

B. 412-73-9648.

* I-698 form = I-698
        application form
        application
        form

A. Let me verify some information on your I-698 form.* Your family name is _____. Is that right?

B. Yes, it is.

A. And your first name is _____. Is that correct?

B. No, it isn't. My first name is _____. My MIDDLE name is _____.

A. I see. Your nationality is _____?

B. Yes. That's right.

A. Born in _____?

B. Yes. That's correct.

A. And is your date of birth _____?

B. No. That's not correct. My date of birth is _____.

A. All right. And what's your social security number?

B. _____.

* I-698 form = I-698
              application form
              application
              form

Practice with another student, using the model dialog above as a guide. Take turns being the INS examiner and the applicant.

CHECK -UP

Questions and Answers

Practice the different ways to ask and answer these questions.

> Is your family name Garcia?
> Your family name is Garcia. Is that right?
> Your family name is Garcia. Is that correct?
> Your family name is Garcia?
>
> | Yes. | No. |
> | --- | --- |
> | Yes, **it is**. | No, **it isn't**. |
> | Yes. That's correct. | No. That's not correct. |
> | Yes. That's right. | No. That's not right. |

Now answer these questions

1. Your native country is Mexico. Is
   that right?
   _____

2. Your telephone number is 241-6289.
   Is that correct?
   _____

3. Is your home in Los Angeles?
   _____

Listening

On Line **A** , write your **place** of birth. On line **B**, write your **date** of birth.

> A. _____   B. _____

*Now listen and circle **A** or **B**.*

1. Ⓐ B   4. A   B
2. A   B   5. A   B
3. A   B   6. A   B

DICTATION

Listen and write.

1. _____

2. _____

CHOICES

Choose the best answer.

> *Example*   My zip code is
> A. 47.
> B. Texas.
> C. 60018.
> D. 060-83-2917.

1. I was born on
   A. Mexico City.
   B. October 3, 1957.
   C. my native country.
   D. California.

2. Houston is in the state of
   A. Texas.
   B. the United States.
   C. Los Angeles.
   D. Mexico.

3. Guatemala is my native
   A. birth.
   B. nationality.
   C. date.
   D. country.

4. 272 Main Street is my current
   A. zip code.
   B. address.
   C. phone number.
   D. social security number.

5. My date of birth is
   A. 1957.
   B. 276-9802.
   C. 7/4/63.
   D. 90047.

REVIEW

Information Exchange

Read these questions and answer them.

> What's your name?
> (Could you spell that, please?)
> What's your nationality?
> What country are you from?
> In what city or town were you born?
> What's your date of birth?

Now interview other students, using these questions. Write the information below.

	Name	Nationality	Country	City or Town	Date of Birth
1.					
2.					
3.					
4.					
5.					

Additional Practice

Ask and answer these questions. Practice with other students.

1. What's the name of your state?
2. What's the name of your city?
3. What's your home address?
4. What's your zip code?
5. What's your home telephone number? Area code first.
6. What's your work phone?
7. What's your native country?
8. What's your place of birth?
9. What's your birth date?

MAPS
GEOGRAPHY
CITIES, STATES, AND CAPITALS
BELIEFS
CERTIFICATE OF SATISFACTORY
    PURSUIT OF A COURSE OF STUDY

A Map of the United States of America
Your Native Country
What State Do You Live In?
I Believe in the United States
Are You Pursuing a Course of Study?

Functional Interview Skills

Reporting Information
Expressing Beliefs
Asking for Clarification
Hesitating
Describing Pursuit of a Course of Study

Grammar

Simple Present Tense
Simple Present Tense vs. To Be
WH-Questions
Yes/No Questions
Short Answers

Related Practice

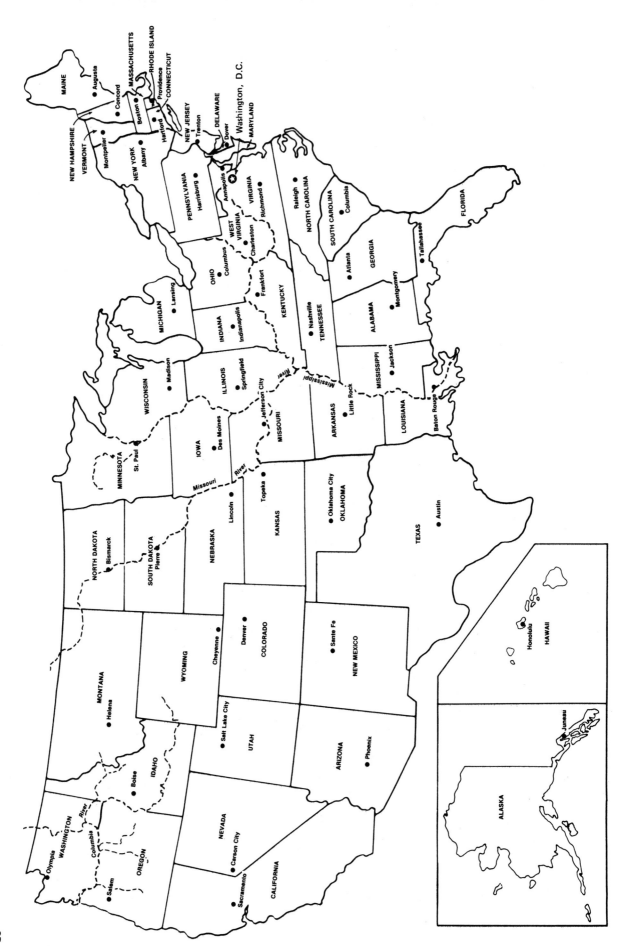

MAINE

Augusta

NEW HAMPSHIRE

VERMONT

Montpelier

Concord

MASSACHUSETTS

Boston

RHODE ISLAND

Providence

CONNECTICUT

Hartford

NEW YORK

Albany

NEW JERSEY

Trenton

DELAWARE

Dover

Washington, D.C.

MARYLAND

Annapolis

PENNSYLVANIA

Harrisburg

WEST VIRGINIA

VIRGINIA

Richmond

Charleston

NORTH CAROLINA

Raleigh

SOUTH CAROLINA

Columbia

OHIO

Columbus

Frankfort

KENTUCKY

MICHIGAN

Lansing

INDIANA

Indianapolis

Nashville

TENNESSEE

GEORGIA

Atlanta

ALABAMA

Montgomery

FLORIDA

Tallahassee

WISCONSIN

Madison

ILLINOIS

Springfield

Jefferson City

MISSOURI

Mississippi River

ARKANSAS

Little Rock

MISSISSIPPI

Jackson

LOUISIANA

Baton Rouge

MINNESOTA

St. Paul

IOWA

Des Moines

Missouri River

Topeka

KANSAS

Lincoln

NEBRASKA

OKLAHOMA

Oklahoma City

NORTH DAKOTA

Bismarck

SOUTH DAKOTA

Pierre

TEXAS

Austin

COLORADO

Denver

Cheyenne

WYOMING

NEW MEXICO

Sante Fe

HAWAII

Honolulu

MONTANA

Helena

UTAH

Salt Lake City

ARIZONA

Phoenix

IDAHO

Boise

ALASKA

Juneau

WASHINGTON

Olympia

Columbia River

OREGON

Salem

NEVADA

Carson City

CALIFORNIA

Sacramento

A Map of the United States of America

This is a map of our country.
It's a map of the United States of America.

The United States is a large country.
The United States is between two other countries.
Canada is north of the United States.
Mexico is south of the United States.

The United States is between two oceans.
The Atlantic Ocean is east of the United States.
The Pacific Ocean is west of the United States.

The capital of the United States is Washington, D.C.
Most temporary residents live in California.
Many other temporary residents live in Texas, Illinois, New York,
     Florida, Arizona, New Jersey, and New Mexico.

What's the name of **your** state?
Point to your state on the map.

What's the name of your state capital?
Point to your state capital on the map.

What's the name of the capital of the United States?
Point to the capital of the United States on the map.

CHECK-UP

Vocabulary Check

north	south	east	west	capital	country

1. The United States is a large _country_.

2. Canada is _____ of the United States.

3. The _____ of the United States is Washington, D.C.

4. The Atlantic Ocean is _____ of the United States.

5. The Pacific Ocean is _____ of the United States.

6. Mexico is _____ of the United States.

Grammar Check

Yes, it is.	No, it isn't.

1. Is the United States a large country?   _Yes, it is._

2. Is the capital of the United States in California?   _____

3. Is Canada north of the United States?   _____

4. Is the Atlantic Ocean west of the United States?   _____

5. Is the United States between Canada and Mexico?   _____

6. Is Washington, D.C. the capital of the United States?   _____

Your Native Country

Draw a map of your native country. On the map, show the capital, show your city or town, and show what is north, south, east, and west of your native country.

Now answer these questions.

1. What's the name of your native country?

   _____

2. What's the capital of your native country?

   _____

3. What city or town are you from?

   _____

4. What is north of your native country? south? east? west?

   _____

   _____

   _____

   _____

   _____

   _____

INTERVIEW
What State Do You Live In?

A. What state do you live in?

B. I live in Texas.

A. What city do you live in?

B. I live in Dallas.

A. Name the capital of the United States.

B. Washington, D.C.

A. And name the capital of your state.

B. Austin.

A. What state do you live in?

B. I live in _____.

A. What city do you live in?

B. I live in _____.

A. Name the capital of the United States.

B. Washington, D.C.

A. And name the capital of your state.

B. _____.

Practice with another student, using the model dialog above as a guide. Take turns being the INS examiner and the applicant.

CHECK-UP

Questions and Answers

Practice the different ways to ask these questions. Then write the answers.

1. What's the name of your state? ⎫
   What state do you live in? ⎭ _____

2. What's the name of your city? ⎫
   What city do you live in? ⎭ _____

> What's the name of _____ ? = Name _____ .

3. What's the name of the capital of the United States? ⎫
   What's the capital of the United States? ⎬
   Name the capital of the United States. ⎭

   _____

4. What's the name of the capital of your state? ⎫
   What's the capital of your state? ⎬
   Name the capital of your state. ⎭

   _____

Listening

On Line **A**, write the name of your state.
On Line **B**, write the name of your state capital.
On Line **C**, write the name of the capital of the United States.

A. _____   B. _____   C. _____

*Now listen and circle **A**, **B**, or **C**.*

1. (A) B   C   4. A   B   C
2. A   B   C   5. A   B   C
3. A   B   C   6. A   B   C

I Believe in the United States

My name is Stanislaw Bienkowski.
I'm applying for permanent residence.
I live in Chicago.
Chicago is a big city in Illinois.

I'm from Poland.
Poland is a communist country.
But I am not a Communist.
I don't believe in Communism.

I believe in the United States.
I believe in the United States government.*
I believe in the United States Constitution.*
I believe in freedom and democracy.

I'm glad I'm in the United States.
I want to be a United States citizen* some day.

* The United States government = the government of the United States.
 The United States Constitution = the Constitution of the United States.
 A United States citizen = a citizen of the United States.

CHECK-UP

Did You Understand?

Answer these questions based on the story.

1. What's his name? _____

2. Where does he live? _____

3. Where is he from? _____

4. Does he believe in Communism? _____

5. What does he believe in? _____

Grammar Check

Yes, I do.	No, I don't.

1. Do you believe in the United States government? $\underline{\text{Yes, I do.}}$

2. Do you believe in Communism? _____

3. Do you believe in the United States Constitution? _____

4. Do you want to be a citizen of the United States some day? _____

Yes, I am. No, I'm not.	Yes, I do. No, I don't.

5. Are you a temporary resident? _____

6. Do you live in Washington, D.C.? _____

7. Are you a Communist? _____

8. Do you believe in the United States government? _____

INTERVIEW
Are You Pursuing a Course of Study?

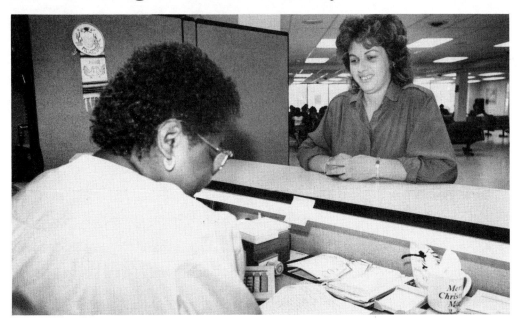

A. Are you pursuing a course of study?

B. I'm sorry. I don't understand. Could you please say that again?

A. Are you going to school now?

B. Yes, I am.

A. Where?

B. At the Community Adult Education Center.

A. Where is that located?

B. Let me see . . . It's on Jefferson Street downtown, next to the library.

A. What are you studying?

B. I'm studying English, and I'm studying the history and government of the United States.

A. Are you enjoying the class?

B. Yes, I am. My teacher is excellent, and I'm learning a lot!

A. Do you have a certificate from the school?

B. Yes, I do. Here you are.

A. Are you pursuing a course of study?

B. I'm sorry. I don't understand. Could you please say that again?

A. Are you going to school now?

B. Yes, I am.

A. Where?

B. At _____.

A. Where is that located?

B. Let me see . . . It's on _____.

A. What are you studying?

B. I'm studying _____.

A. Are you enjoying the class?

B. Yes, I am. My teacher is excellent, and I'm learning a lot!

A. Do you have a certificate from the school?

B. Yes, I do. Here you are.

Practice with another student, using the model dialog above as a guide. Take turns being the INS examiner and the applicant.

CHECK-UP

Vocabulary Check

course	understand	certificate	history	school	studying

1. Are you pursuing a _____*course*_____ of study?

2. I'm _____ English at the Adult Education Center.

3. The _____ is on Main Street downtown.

4. I'm also studying United States government and _____.

5. I have a _____ from the school.

6. I'm sorry. I don't _____.

Grammar Check

am	is	are

1. My teacher _____*is*_____ excellent.

2. I _____ not a Communist.

3. Where _____ the school located?

4. What _____ you studying?

5. The state capital of California _____ Sacramento.

6. I _____ a temporary resident.

DICTATION

1. _____

2. _____

CHOICES

Choose the best answer.

> *Example*   Los Angeles is a large
>   A. country.
>   (B.) city.
>   C. state.
>   D. ocean.

1. The United States is a large
   A. state.
   B. ocean.
   C. country.
   D. city.

2. The capital of the United States is
   A. Austin.
   B. Sacramento.
   C. Albany.
   D. Washington, D.C.

3. Mexico is
   A. north of the United States.
   B. south of the United States.
   C. east of the United States.
   D. west of the United States.

4. Canada is
   A. north of the United States.
   B. south of the United States.
   C. east of the United States.
   D. west of the United States.

5. The Atlantic Ocean is
   A. north of the United States.
   B. south of the United States.
   C. east of the United States.
   D. west of the United States.

6. Some day I want to be a United States
   A. government.
   B. Constitution.
   C. capital.
   D. citizen.

REVIEW

Ask and answer these questions. Practice with other students.

1. What's your name?

2. Where are you from?

3. What's your date of birth?

4. What's your social security number?

5. What's your alien registration number?

6. What state do you live in?

7. What city do you live in?

8. What's your home address?

9. What's your home telephone number?

10. Name the capital of your state.

11. Name the capital of the United States.

12. Do you believe in Communism?

13. Do you believe in the United States Constitution?

14. Do you want to be a citizen of the United States some day?

15. Are you pursuing a course of study?

16. Where?

17. What are you studying?

18. Do you have a certificate?

THE FLAG

The Flag of the United States
Your Native Country's Flag
How Many Stars Does the American Flag Have?
The Pledge of Allegiance

Functional Interview Skills

Reporting Information
Asking for Repetition
Hesitating

Grammar

There Is/There Are
Singular/Plural
Have/Has

Related Practice

The Flag of the United States

There are three colors on the flag of the United States.
The flag is red, white, and blue.

There are fifty states in the United States.
There are fifty stars on the American flag.
There is one star for each state.

There are thirteen stripes on the American flag.
The stripes are red and white.
There are seven red stripes and six white stripes.
There is one stripe for each of the first thirteen states
      in the United States.
The first thirteen states were called colonies.

CHECK-UP

Did You Understand?

Answer these questions based on the story. Use full sentences.

1. What are the colors of the American flag?

   _____

2. How many states are there in the United States?

   _____

3. How many stars are there on the American flag?

   _____

4. How many stripes are there on the flag?

   _____

5. What colors are the stripes?

   _____

Vocabulary Check

stripes	red	colors	colonies	blue	stars

1. The American flag is red, white, and _____blue_____.

2. There are thirteen _____ on the American flag.

3. There are fifty _____ on the American flag.

4. There are three _____ on the flag of the United States.

5. The stripes on the flag are _____ and white.

6. The first thirteen states were called _____.

GRAMMAR CHECK

There is	There are

1. __There are__ fifty states in the United States.

2. _____ one star for each state.

3. _____ fifty stars on the American flag.

4. _____ thirteen stripes on the flag.

5. _____ one stripe for each of the first thirteen colonies.

6. _____ seven red stripes and six white stripes.

Your Native Country's Flag

Draw the flag of your native country.

Now answer the questions.

1. How many colors are there on your native country's flag?

   _____

2. What are the colors of the flag?

   _____

3. Describe the flag. What's on it?

   _____

   _____

   _____

INTERVIEW

How Many Stars Does the American Flag Have?

A. How many stars does the American flag have?

B. I'm sorry. Could you please repeat the question?

A. Certainly. How many stars does the American flag have?

B. Uh . . . let me see. It has fifty stars.

A. That's right.

A. How many _____ does the American flag have?

B. I'm sorry. Could you please repeat the question?

A. Certainly. How many _____ does the American flag have?

B. Uh . . . let me see. It has _____ _____ .

A. That's right.

Practice these exercises with another student, using the model dialog above as a guide. Take turns being the INS examiner and the applicant.

1. stripes
    thirteen

2. colors
    three

CHECK-UP

Questions and Answers

Practice the different ways to ask and answer these questions.

How many colors are there on the American flag?	=	How many colors does the American flag have?
There are three colors on the American flag.	=	The American flag has three colors.

Now answer these questions using full sentences.

1. How many stripes does the American flag have?

   _____

2. How many stripes are there on the American flag?

   _____

3. How many stars does the American flag have?

   _____

4. How many states are there in the United States?

   _____

Listening

Listen and circle the correct answer.

1.
50
13

3.
13
3

5.
red and white
red, white, and blue

2.
50
13

4.
stripes
colonies

6.
red and white
red, white, and blue

DICTATION

1. _____

2. _____

CHOICES

Choose the best answer.

Example   The flag of the United States has
A. two colors.
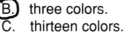 B. three colors.
C. thirteen colors.
D. fifty colors.

1. The colors of the American flag are
    A. red and white.
    B. red and blue.
    C. red, white, and brown.
    D. red, white, and blue.

2. The American flag has one star for each
    A. city.
    B. state.
    C. citizen.
    D. colony.

3. The American flag has
    A. two stripes.
    B. three stripes.
    C. thirteen stripes.
    D. fifty stripes.

4. The flag of the United States has
    A. three stars.
    B. thirteen stars.
    C. fifty stars.
    D. one hundred stars.

5. The first thirteen states were called
    A. capitals.
    B. colonies.
    C. countries.
    D. citizens.

The Pledge of Allegiance

I pledge allegiance
to the flag
of the United States of America,
and to the republic
for which it stands,
one nation,
under God,
indivisible,
with liberty
and justice
for all.

BRANCHES OF GOVERNMENT

Branches of Government
Making, Enforcing, and Explaining
the Laws of the United States
How Many Branches Does
the United States Government Have?

Functional Interview Skills

Reporting Information
Checking Understanding
Hesitating

Grammar

Simple Present Tense
Have/Has
Can

Related Practice

ExpressWays Foundations: Chapter 5
ExpressWays Book One: Chapter 5
Side by Side Second Edition Book 1: Chapter 11
Side by Side First Edition Book 1A: Chapter 11

Branches of Government

The government of the United States has three parts.
These parts are called the three branches of government.

The names of the three branches of government are
    the legislative branch,
    the executive branch,
    and the judicial branch.

Senators and representatives work in the legislative branch.
The President and the Vice President work in the executive branch.
The Supreme Court justices work in the judicial branch.

CHECK-UP

Vocabulary Check

branches	legislative	government	judicial	executive

1. The ___government___ of the United States has three parts.

2. There are three _____ of government in the United States.

3. The President works in the _____ branch of the government.

4. Senators and representatives work in the _____ branch.

5. The Supreme Court justices work in the _____ branch.

Did You Understand?

Answer these questions based on the story. Use full sentences.

1. How many branches of government are there in the United States?

    _____

2. What are the names of the branches of government?

    _____

3. Who works in the executive branch?

    _____

4. Who works in the judicial branch?

    _____

5. Who works in the legislative branch?

    _____

Making, Enforcing, and Explaining the Laws of the United States

The legislative branch of the government is called the Congress.

Senators and representatives are in the Congress.

They make the laws of the United States.

They work in the Capitol.*

The Capitol is in Washington, D.C.

The President and the Vice President work in the executive branch.

They enforce the laws of the United States.

The President lives and works in the White House.

The White House is in Washington, D.C.

The Supreme Court justices work in the judicial branch.

They explain the laws of the United States.

They work in the Supreme Court.

The Supreme Court is in Washington, D.C.

*The Capitol = the U.S. Capitol, the United States Capitol.

56

CHECK-UP

Matching I

1. senators and representatives ⟍   the judicial branch

2. the President and the Vice President ⟍ the legislative branch

3. the Supreme Court justices   the executive branch

Matching II

1. the executive branch   makes the laws

2. the judicial branch   enforces the laws

3. the legislative branch   explains the laws

Matching III

1. the Supreme Court   the executive branch

2. the White House   the legislative branch

3. the Capitol   the judicial branch

Answer These Questions

1. Who makes the laws of the United States?

   _____

2. Who explains the laws of the United States?

   _____

3. Who enforces the laws of the United States?

   _____

INTERVIEW

How Many Branches Does the United States Government Have?

A. How many branches does the United States government have?

B. The government has three branches.

A. Can you name the three branches?

B. Yes, I can. The legislative branch, the executive branch, and the judicial branch.

A. And which branch makes the laws of the United States?

B. Which branch makes the laws?

A. Yes.

B. Hmm. I think the legislative branch makes the laws.

A. That's right. And can you tell me who works in the legislative branch?

B. The senators and representatives.

A. That's correct. Very good.

A. How many branches does the United States government have?

B. The government has three branches.

A. Can you name the three branches?

B. Yes, I can. The legislative branch, the executive branch, and the judicial branch.

A. And which branch _____ the laws of the United States?

B. Which branch _____ the laws?

A. Yes.

B. Hmm. I think the _____ branch _____ the laws.

A. That's right. And can you tell me who works in the _____ branch?

B. _____.

A. That's correct. Very good.

Practice with another student, using the model dialog above as a guide. Take turns being the INS examiner and the applicant.

1. enforces
    executive
    the President and the
        Vice President

2. explains
    judicial
    the Supreme Court justices

CHECK-UP

Grammar Check

Circle the correct answer.

1. The President (live   (lives)) in the White House.

2. Senators (work   works) in the Capitol.

3. The Vice President (work   works) in the executive branch.

4. The Supreme Court justices (explain   explains) the laws.

5. The President (enforce   enforces) the laws.

Questions and Answers

Practice the different ways to ask these questions. Then write the answers.

1. Which branch of the government makes the laws? }
   Which branch of the government does the Congress work in? }

   _____

2. Which branch of the government explains the laws? }
   Which branch of the government does the Supreme Court work in? }

   _____

3. Which branch of the government enforces the laws? }
   Which branch of the government does the President work in? }

   _____

Listening

Listen and circle the correct answer.

1. (White House)   Capitol   4. Congress   Supreme Court
2. White House   Capitol   5. senators   the President
3. Congress   Supreme Court 6. senators   the President

DICTATION

1. _____

2. _____

CHOICES

Choose the best answer.

Example   The government of the United States has three
    A. senators.
    B. presidents.
    Ⓒ branches.
    D. laws.

1. The three branches of the United States government are the legislative, the executive, and
    A. the representatives.
    B. the senators.
    C. the White House.
    D. the judicial.

2. The President of the United States works in
    A. the White House.
    B. the Capitol.
    C. the Supreme Court.
    D. the legislative branch.

3. The Supreme Court
    A. makes the laws.
    B. enforces the laws.
    C. explains the laws.
    D. lives in the White House.

4. United States senators and representatives work in
    A. the Supreme Court.
    B. the executive branch.
    C. the judicial branch.
    D. the legislative branch.

5. The Congress of the United States
    A. makes the laws.
    B. enforces the laws.
    C. explains the laws.
    D. lives in the White House.

REVIEW

Ask and answer these questions. Practice with other students.

1. What's your family name?

2. How do you spell it?

3. What's your social security number?

4. What city or town do you live in?

5. Name the capital of your state.

6. Name the capital of the United States.

7. Are you a Communist?

8. Do you believe in the government of the United States?

9. Are you going to school now?

10. What's the name of your school?

11. How many states are there in the United States?

12. How many stripes does the American flag have?

13. What are the colors of the American flag?

14. Who makes the laws of the United States?

15. Where does the President live?

16. How many branches of government does the United States have?

17. Name the branches of government in the United States.

18. What does the Supreme Court do?

THE CONGRESS
THE PRESIDENT
THE SUPREME COURT

The Congress of the United States
Who Makes the Laws of the United States?
The President of the United States
The Supreme Court
Are You Attending Classes Now?

Functional Interview Skills

Reporting Information
Describing Pursuit of a Course of Study

Grammar

Simple Present Tense vs. To Be
There Are
Time Expressions
Question Formation

Related Practice

ExpressWays Foundations: Chapter 6
ExpressWays Book One: Chapter 6
Side by Side Second Edition Book 1: Chapters 12, 13
Side by Side First Edition Book 1A: Chapters 12, 13

The Congress of the United States

The Congress of the United States is the legislative branch of the government.
The legislative branch makes the laws of the United States.
The Congress has two parts: the Senate and the House of Representatives.

Senators work in the Senate.
There are one hundred senators.
There are two senators from each state.
A senator's term is six years.

Representatives work in the House of Representatives.
Representatives are also called congressmen and congresswomen.
There are 435 representatives.
There are different numbers of representatives from different states.
States with many people have more representatives.
States with fewer people have fewer representatives.
A representative's term is two years.

CHECK-UP

Vocabulary Check

representatives	senators	congresswomen	two
	legislative	six	

1. The Congress is the ___**legislative**___ branch of the government.

2. There are one hundred _____ in the U.S. Senate.

3. There are 435 _____ in the Congress.

4. A senator's term is _____ years.

5. A representative's term is _____ years.

6. Congressmen and _____ work in the House of Representatives.

Did You Understand?

Answer these questions. Use short answers.

1. Who makes the laws of the United States?

   _____

2. What are the two parts of the Congress called?

   _____

   _____

3. How many senators are there in the United States Senate?

   _____

4. How many representatives are there in the House of Representatives?

   _____

5. How many representatives are there from your state in the U.S. House of Representatives?

   _____

6. How long is a senator's term?

   _____

7. How long is a representative's term?

   _____

INTERVIEW

Who Makes the Laws of the United States?

A. Now I want to ask you some questions about government.

B. All right.

A. Who makes the laws of the United States?

B. The Congress.

A. And what are the two parts of the Congress called?

B. The Senate and the House of Representatives.

A. Can you name the two United States senators from your state?

B. Yes. They're _____ and _____.

A. And do you know the name of your congressman in the House of Representatives?

B. Yes. It's _____.

Practice with another student. Take turns being the INS examiner and the applicant.

The President of the United States

The President of the United States is the head of the executive branch of the government.

The executive branch enforces the laws of the United States.

The President is the chief executive.

The President is Commander-in-Chief of the armed forces.

The President lives and works in the White House.

The President's term is four years.

The American people elect a president every four years.

The President can serve two terms.

The Vice President works with the President.

The American people elect the President and the Vice President at the same time.

If the President dies, the Vice President becomes the new President.

The name of the President of the United States is _____.

The name of the Vice President is _____.

CHECK-UP

Vocabulary Check

White House	serve	armed forces	executive	elect

1. The President lives in the __White House__ .

2. The American people _____ a president every four years.

3. The President is Commander-in-Chief of the _____ .

4. The President can _____ two terms.

5. The President is the head of the _____ branch of the government.

The Answer is "The President!"

Practice these questions and write the answers.

1. Who is the chief executive of the United States?

   _____

2. Who is the Commander-in-Chief of the armed forces?

   _____

3. Who lives in the White House?

   _____

4. Who is the head of the executive branch of the government?

   _____

Fill in the Numbers

1. A U.S. senator's term is __6__ years.

2. A representative's term is _____ years.

3. The President can serve _____ terms.

4. Americans elect a president every _____ years.

5. There are _____ United States senators.

6. There are _____ representatives in the Congress.

The Supreme Court

The Supreme Court and other federal courts are the
    judicial branch of the government.
The judicial branch explains the laws of the United States.
The Supreme Court is the highest court in the United States.

There are nine judges in the Supreme Court.
They are also called Supreme Court justices.
They serve for life.
The American people don't elect the Supreme Court justices.
The President appoints them, and the Senate approves them.

The head of the Supreme Court is the Chief Justice of
    the United States.
The name of the Chief Justice of the United States is

_____ .

CHECK-UP

Did You Understand?

1. What is the highest court in the United States?

   _____

2. Which branch of government is it in?

   _____

3. How many judges are there in the Supreme Court?

   _____

4. Who appoints the Supreme Court justices?

   _____

5. Who is the head of the Supreme Court?

   _____

6. What is the name of the Chief Justice of the United States?

   _____

Grammar Check

Fill in the blanks.

Where	What	How long	How many	Who

1. __How many__ senators are there in the Senate?

2. _____ is a representative's term?

3. _____ makes the laws of the United States?

4. _____ is the name of the Vice President?

5. _____ does the Congress work?

Now answer the questions.

Questions and Answers

Practice the different ways to ask these questions.

> Who's the Chief Justice of the United States?
> Name the Chief Justice of the United States.
> What's the name of the Chief Justice of the United States?
> Can you name the Chief Justice of the United States?

Now answer these questions.

1. Who's the President of the United States? _____

2. Name the Vice President of the United States. _____

3. What's the name of your representative in Congress? _____

4. Can you name the two U.S. senators from your state? _____

   _____

5. Who's the Chief Justice of the United States? _____

Listening

On Line **A**, write the name of the President of the United States.
On Line **B**, write the name of one senator from your state.
On Line **C**, write the name of the Chief Justice of the United States.

A. _____   B. _____   C. _____

*Now listen and circle **A**, **B**, or **C**.*

1. (A) B   C   4. A   B   C
2. A   B   C   5. A   B   C
3. A   B   C   6. A   B   C

INTERVIEW

Are You Attending Classes Now?

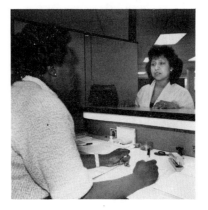

A. Are you attending classes now?

B. Yes, I am. I'm studying English and U.S. history and government at the Adult Education Center.

A. How often do you go there?

B. Twice a week.*

A. When are your classes?

B. My classes are on Monday and Wednesday from 7 P.M. to 9 P.M.

A. And how many hours have you studied so far?

B. Forty hours.

*once a week
  twice a week
  three times a week
  four times a week
  five times a week

A. Are you attending classes now?

B. Yes, I am. I'm studying _____
   at _____.

A. How often do you go there?

B. _____.

A. When are your classes?

B. My classes are on _____ from _____ to _____.

A. And how many hours have you studied so far?

B. _____ hours.

Practice with another student. Take turns being the INS examiner and the applicant.

DICTATION

1. _____

2. _____

CHOICES

Choose the best answer.

Example   A United States senator's term is
    A. two years.
    B. four years.
    Ⓒ six years.
    D. eight years.

1. There are 435 congressmen and congresswomen in
   A. the White House.
   B. the House of Representatives.
   C. the Senate.
   D. the Supreme Court.

2. The two parts of the United States Congress are the House of Representatives and
   A. the White House.
   B. the Capitol.
   C. the Supreme Court.
   D. the Senate.

3. The President of the United States is
   A. the head of the legislative branch.
   B. the Chief Justice.
   C. the Chief Executive.
   D. the head of the judicial branch.

4. The American people elect a president
   A. every two years.
   B. every four years.
   C. every six years.
   D. if the President dies.

5. The American people don't elect
   A. Supreme Court justices.
   B. senators.
   C. representatives.
   D. the President and the Vice President.

REVIEW

Review Chart: Branches of Government

	Legislative Branch		Executive Branch	Judicial Branch
	Senators	Representatives	President	Supreme Court Justices
Number	100	435	1	9
Term	6 years	2 years	4 years	life
Place of Work	Senate	House of Representatives	White House	Supreme Court
Job	Make the laws.		Enforce the laws.	Explain the laws.

Study the chart. Then practice with another student, asking and answering questions based on the information.

Who works in the _____ branch of the government?
How many _____s are there?
How long is _____'s term?
Where do/does _____ work?
What does _____ do?

Now ask and answer questions about the names of people in the government.

Who's _____?
Name _____.
What's the name of _____?
Can you name _____?

TYPES OF GOVERNMENT
STATE AND LOCAL GOVERNMENT
PUBLIC OFFICIALS
THE CONSTITUTION
THE BILL OF RIGHTS

A Representative Form of Government
State and Local Government
What City or Town Do You Live In?
The Constitution
The Bill of Rights

Functional Interview Skills

Reporting Information

Grammar

Review:
To Be
Simple Present Tense
Have/Has
There Are
Can
WH-Questions
Yes/No Questions

Related Practice

ExpressWays Foundations: Chapter 7
ExpressWays Book One: Chapter 7
Side by Side Second Edition Book 1: Chapter 14
Side by Side First Edition Book 1A: Chapter 14

A Representative Form of Government

The United States is not a dictatorship.
It doesn't have a dictator.
The United States is not a monarchy.
It doesn't have a king or a queen.

The United States is a republic.
It has a democratic form of government.
It has a representative form of government.

The American people elect representatives.
They elect the President, the Vice President, the senators, and the
      congressmen and congresswomen.
These officials work in the United States government.
They serve the American people.

CHECK-UP

Vocabulary Check

elect	monarchy	democratic	republic	serve

1. The United States has a __*democratic*__ form of government.

2. The American people _____ representatives.

3. These representatives _____ in the government.

4. The United States isn't a dictatorship or _____.

5. The United States is a _____.

Did You Understand?

Answer these questions.

1. What kind of government does the United States have?

   _____

2. Is the United States a monarchy, a dictatorship, or a republic?

   _____

3. Who elects the President and the Vice President of the United States?

   _____

4. What officials do the American people elect?

   _____

How About You?

What form of government is there in your native country?
Do the people elect officials? Who?

State and Local Government

There are three levels of government in the United States:
federal, state, and local.

The federal government has three branches.
Most state governments also have three branches.

The state legislature makes the laws of the state.
The state courts explain the laws of the state.
The governor is the head of the state's government.
The governor enforces the laws of the state.
The name of our state is _____.
The name of our governor is _____.

There are many kinds of local government.
There are cities, towns, and counties.
In some cities and towns, a mayor is the head of the local
government.
Other cities and towns have a city manager.
The name of our city/town is _____.
The name of our mayor/city manager is _____.
The name of our county is _____.

CHECK-UP

Vocabulary Check

state courts	mayor	governor	state legislature	local

1. The three levels of government in the United States are federal, state,

   and _____local_____ .

2. The head of a state's government is the _____ .

3. The head of a city's government is the _____ or city manager.

4. The _____ makes the laws of the state.

5. The _____ explain the laws of the state.

Did You Understand?

Answer these questions.

1. What's the head of a state's government called?

   _____

2. Who makes the laws of your state?

   _____

3. What's the head of your city or town's government called?

   _____

4. What are the three levels of government in the United States?

   _____

5. What are the three branches of government in the United States?

   _____

INTERVIEW
What City or Town Do You Live In?

A.   What city or town do you live in?

B.   I live in Anaheim.

A.   Who makes the laws in Anaheim?

B.   The City Council.

A.   And what's the leader of the government in Anaheim called?

B.   The mayor.

A.   Do you know the mayor's name?

B.   Yes. It's _____.*

A.   What county do you live in?

B.   Orange County.

A.   And who makes the laws in Orange County?

B.   The Board of Supervisors.

A.   Can you name the governor of your state?

B.   Yes. It's Governor _____.†

*Use a student's name here, unless you live in Anaheim.
†If you don't live in California, use a student's name.

A. What city or town do you live in?

B. _____.

A. Who makes the laws in _____?

B. _____.

A. And what's the leader of the government in _____ called?

B. The _____.

A. Do you know the _____'s name?

B. Yes. It's _____.

A. What county do you live in?

B. _____.

A. And who makes the laws in _____?

B. _____.

A. Can you name the governor of your state?

B. Yes. It's Governor _____.

Practice with another student, using the model dialog above as a guide. Take turns being the INS examiner and the applicant.

The Constitution

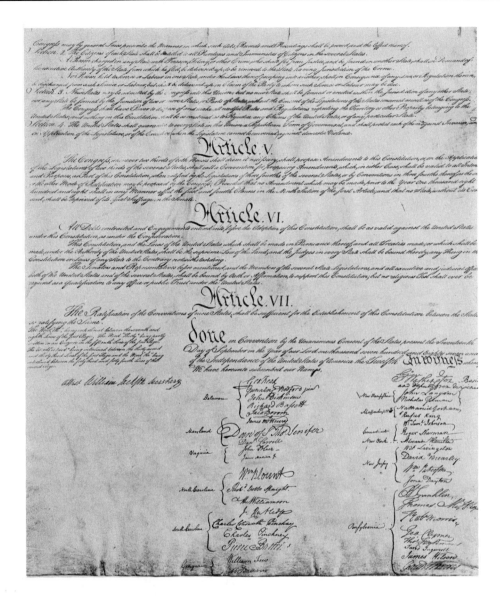

The Constitution is the highest law in the United States.
It is called "the supreme law of the land."

The Constitution gives the rules for the three branches of government.
It says what each branch can do and what each branch cannot do.
It tells the Senate and the House of Representatives how to make laws.
It tells the President and the Vice President how to enforce the laws.
It helps the Supreme Court and other courts explain the laws.
The Constitution also says that states can make their own laws.

The Bill of Rights

The people of the United States can change the Constitution.
Changes in the Constitution are called amendments.
There are 26 amendments to the Constitution.

The first ten amendments are called the Bill of Rights.
The Bill of Rights gives rights and freedoms to all people in the United States.

The first amendment gives Americans many important rights.
It guarantees freedom of speech.
(Americans can say what they want to.)
It guarantees freedom of the press.
(Americans can write what they want to.)
It guarantees freedom of religion.
(Americans can worship as they want to.)
It guarantees freedom of assembly.
(Americans can meet together as they want to.)

CHECK-UP

"Mirror" Questions

Practice these questions. Notice that they ask about the same thing.

What is the highest law in the United States? The Constitution.	What is the Constitution? The highest law in the United States.

Answer these "mirror" questions on a separate sheet of paper. Then practice asking and answering these questions with other students.

1. What are changes in the Constitution of the United States called?
2. What are amendments?

3. What are the first ten amendments to the Constitution called?
4. What is the Bill of Rights?

5. What is the supreme law of the land?
6. What is the Constitution of the United States?

Answer These Questions

1. Can the American people change the Constitution? _____

2. How many amendments are there to the Constitution? _____

3. Which amendment to the Constitution guarantees freedom of religion? _____

Bill of Rights Practice

These are very common interview questions about the Bill of Rights. Practice asking and answering them with another student.

1. Name one right guaranteed by the Bill of Rights.

2. Name two rights guaranteed by the first amendment to the Constitution.

3. Name three rights included in the Bill of Rights.

4. Name four rights guaranteed by the Bill of Rights.

5. Name some rights included in the first amendment to the Constitution.

DICTATION

1. _____

2. _____

Choices

Choose the best answer.

Example   The head of a state's government is
     A. the mayor.
     (B.) the governor.
     C. the city manager.
     D. the President.

1. The United States is
   A. a republic.
   B. a monarchy.
   C. a dictatorship.
   D. a legislature.

2. Many cities and towns in the United States have
   A. a governor.
   B. a mayor.
   C. a president.
   D. a vice president.

3. The first ten amendments to the U.S. Constitution are called
   A. the branches of government.
   B. the levels of government.
   C. the House of Representatives.
   D. the Bill of Rights.

4. The three levels of government in the United States are
   A. cities, towns, and counties.
   B. the legislative, the executive, and the judicial.
   C. federal, state, and local.
   D. monarchies, dictatorships, and republics.

5. The Bill of Rights
   A. tells the Congress how to make laws.
   B. tells the President how to enforce laws.
   C. tells the American people how to elect representatives.
   D. gives rights and freedoms to all people in the United States.

REVIEW

Listen Carefully!

These questions sound the same, but they are very different. Listen carefully and circle the correct answer.

1.
> the Constitution
>
> (the Supreme Court)

2.
> the Constitution
>
> the Supreme Court

3.
> federal, state, and local
>
> legislative, executive, and judicial

4.
> federal, state, and local
>
> legislative, executive, and judicial

5.
> the executive branch
>
> the judicial branch

6.
> the executive branch
>
> the judicial branch

Additional Practice

Ask and answer these questions. Practice with other students.

1. What city or town do you live in?
2. What county do you live in?
3. What state do you live in?
4. Name the governor of your state.
5. Who makes the laws of your state?
6. Who makes the laws of the United States?
7. How many senators are there in the United States Senate?
8. Can you name the two United States senators from your state?
9. How many representatives are there in the U.S. House of Representatives?
10. How many congressmen are there from your state in the U.S. House of Representatives?
11. What's the name of your congressperson in the House of Representatives?
12. Who's the Chief Justice of the United States?
13. What's the name of the President of the United States?
14. Can you name the Vice President of the United States?

SONGS OF FREEDOM

The Star-Spangled Banner
(The National Anthem)

Oh, say, can you see,
by the dawn's early light,
What so proudly we hailed
at the twilight's last gleaming;
Whose broad stripes and bright stars,
through the perilous fight
O'er the ramparts we watched,
were so gallantly streaming;
And the rocket's red glare,
the bombs bursting in air,
Gave proof through the night
that our flag was still there.
Oh, say, does the star-spangled
banner yet wave
O'er the land of the free
and the home of the brave?

—Francis Scott Key

America, The Beautiful

O beautiful for spacious skies,
for amber waves of grain,
For purple mountain majesties,
above the fruited plain!
America! America!
God shed His grace on thee,
And crown thy good with brotherhood,
from sea to shining sea!

—Katharine Lee Bates

INFORMATION FOR TEMPORARY RESIDENTS

After you are a Temporary Resident for 18 months, you must apply for
Permanent Residence.

You have one year to apply for Permanent Residence.

You **must** apply for Permanent Residence before the expiration date on your
Temporary Resident Card.

While you are a Temporary Resident, you may not leave the United States for
more than 30 days at a time, and you may not be absent from the country
more than a total of 90 days.

You must not be convicted of a felony or three misdemeanors.

You must not receive certain types of public cash assistance (welfare).

You must notify INS if you move.

For more information, call the following toll-free numbers:

INS:
  1-800-777-7700

NALEO (National Association of Latino Elected & Appointed Officials):
  1-800-44-NALEO
  1-800-34-NALEO (In California only)

SCRIPTS FOR LISTENING EXERCISES

Page 7

Listen and circle the correct answer.

1. A. Could you spell your family name, please?
   B. M-A-R-T-I-N-E-Z.
2. A. Could you spell your last name, please?
   B. S-A-N-T-O-S.
3. A. Could you spell your surname, please?
   B. T-R-A-N.
4. A. How do you spell your last name?
   B. C-R-U-Z.
5. A. How do you spell your family name?
   B. W-O-N-G.

Page 7

Listen and write the name you hear.

1. A. What's your family name?
   B. Garcia.
   A. Could you spell that, please?
   B. G-A-R-C-I-A.
2. A. What's your last name?
   B. Lam.
   A. Could you spell that, please?
   B. L-A-M.
3. A. What's your surname?
   B. Perez.
   A. Could you spell that, please?
   B. P-E-R-E-Z.
4. A. What's your last name?
   B. Cheng.
   A. How do you spell that?
   B. C-H-E-N-G.
5. A. What's your family name?
   B. Velasquez.
   A. How do you spell that?
   B. V-E-L-A-S-Q-U-E-Z.
6. A. What's your surname?
   B. Gudarski.
   A. Please spell it.
   B. G-U-D-A-R-S-K-I.

Page 11

Listen and circle the number you hear.

1. My address is thirty Main Street.
2. My address is thirteen Spring Street.
3. My address is fifty Stanley Avenue.
4. My address is forty-six fifteen Donaldson Street.
5. My address is eighteen thirty-nine Parkman Avenue.
6. My address is eight forty-two Conway Avenue.

Page 28

*Listen and circle **A** or **B**.*

1. Where were you born?
2. What's your date of birth?

3. What's your place of birth?
4. When were you born?
5. Where are you from?
6. What's your birth date?

Page 37

*Listen and circle **A**, **B**, or **C**.*

1. What's the name of your state?
2. Name the capital of the United States.
3. What's the name of your state capital?
4. What state do you live in?
5. Name the capital of your state.
6. What's the capital of the United States?

Page 50

Listen and circle the correct answer.

1. How many states are there in the United States?
2. How many stripes does the American flag have?
3. How many colors does the American flag have?
4. What were the first thirteen states called?
5. What are the colors of the American flag?
6. What colors are the stripes on the flag of the United States?

Page 60

Listen and circle the correct answer.

1. Where does the President work?
2. Where does the Congress work?
3. Who makes the laws of the United States?
4. Who explains the laws of the United States?
5. Who enforces the laws of the United States?
6. Who works in the Congress of the United States?

Page 71

*Listen and circle **A**, **B**, or **C**.*

1. Who's the Commander-in-Chief of the armed forces?
2. Who works in the Congress of the United States?
3. Who explains the laws of the United States?
4. Who works in the White House?
5. Who makes the laws of the United States?
6. Who don't the American people elect?

Page 86

These questions sound the same, but they are very different. Listen carefully and circle the correct answer.

1. What's the highest court in the United States?
2. What's the highest law in the United States?
3. What are the three levels of government in the United States?
4. What are the three branches of the United States government?
5. Which branch of government enforces the laws?
6. Which branch of government explains the laws?

SENTENCES FOR DICTATION EXERCISES

Page 14

1. I am applying for amnesty.
2. The United States of America is my new home.

Page 29

1. My home is in _____.
   (name of city or town)
2. I am living in the United States of America.

Page 42

1. I want to be a citizen of the United States.
2. I am studying English at school.

Page 51

1. There are fifty states in the United States.

2. The American flag is red, white, and blue.

Page 61

1. The President of the United States lives in the White House.
2. The White House is in Washington, D.C.

Page 73

1. I am going to school today.
2. I'm studying about the President of the United States.

Page 85

1. I am studying the Constitution of the United States.
2. The Constitution gives rights to all people in the United States.

TEXT READINGS IN SPANISH

Capítulo 1

Página 2   Residente Temporal

Mi nombre es Carlos Rivera.
Mi nombre es Carlos.
Mi apellido es Rivera.

Yo soy residente temporal.
Yo estoy aplicando para la amnistía.
Yo estoy aplicando para la residencia permanente.

Página 4   Tarjeta de Residente Temporal

Yo soy residente temporal.
Esta es mi tarjeta de residente temporal.

Mi apellido es Rivera.
Mi nombre es Carlos.
Mi segundo nombre es Manuel.
Mi nombre completo es Carlos Manuel Rivera.

Yo estoy aplicando para la amnistía.
Yo estoy aplicando para la residencia permanente.

Página 8   Números

Esta es mi tarjeta de residente temporal.
Mi número de registro extranjero es A-92475816.

Esta es mi tarjeta de Seguro Social.
Mi numero de Seguro Social es 408-37-1692.

Esta es mi número de teléfono.
Mi número de teléfono es 257-9108.

Página 10   Mi Dirección

Mi dirección es 80 Stanley Avenue.
Mi número de departamento es 12-D.
El nombre de mi ciudad es Los Angeles.
El nombre de mi estado es California.
Los Angeles está en California.
California está en los Estados Unidos de Norteamérica.
Mi código postal es 90048.

Yo estoy aplicando para la amnistía.
Yo estoy aplicando para la residencia permanente en los
     Estados Unidos de Norteamérica.

Capítulo 2

Página 18   Yo nací en Monterrey

Mi nombre es María López.
Yo soy de México.
Ahora yo estoy en los Estados Unidos de Norteamérica.
El nombre de mi ciudad es Houston.
Houston está en el estado de Texas.
Texas es un estado en los Estados Unidos.

Yo soy Mexicana.
Yo nací en Monterrey.
Monterrey está en el estado de Nuevo León.
Nuevo León es un estado en México.

Yo nací el 4 de Mayo 1962.
El nombre de mi madre es Gloria.
El nombre de mi padre es Oscar.
Mi madre y mi padre están en Monterrey.
Yo no estoy en Monterrey.
Yo estoy en Houston.
Yo estoy aplicando para la residencia permanente en los
     Estados Unidos de Norteamérica.

Capítulo 3

Página 33   Un Mapa de los Estados Unidos
                         de Norteamérica

Este es un mapa de nuestro país.
Es un mapa de los Estados Unidos de Norteamérica.

Los Estados Unidos es un país grande.
Los Estados Unidos está entre dos otros países.
Canadá está al norte de los Estados Unidos.
México está al sur de los Estados Unidos.

Los Estados Unidos está entre dos océanos.
El océano Atlántico está al este de los Estados Unidos.
El océano Pácifico está al oeste de los Estados Unidos.

La capital de los Estados Unidos es Washington, D.C.
La mayor parte de los residentes temporales viven en California.
Muchos otros residentes temporales viven en Texas, Illinois,
     Nueva York, Florida, Arizona, Nueva Jersey y Nuevo Mexico.

Cuál es el nombre de su estado?
Señale su estado en el mapa.

Cuál es el nombre de la capital de su estado?
Señale la capital de su estado en el mapa.

Cuál es el nombre de la capital de los Estados Unidos?
Señale la capital de los Estados Unidos en el mapa.

Página 38   Yo creo en los Estados Unidos

Mi nombre es Stanislaw Bienkowski.
Yo estoy aplicando para la residencia permanente.
Yo vivo en Chicago.
Chicago es una ciudad grande en Illinois.

Yo soy de Polonia.
Polonia es un país comunista.
Pero yo no soy comunista.
Yo no creo en el comunismo.

Yo creo en los Estados Unidos.
Yo creo en el gobierno de los Estados Unidos.
Yo creo en la constitución de los Estados Unidos.
Yo creo en libertad y democracia.

Yo estoy feliz de estar en los Estados Unidos.
Yo quiero ser ciudadano de los Estados Unidos algún día.

Capítulo 4

Página 46   La Bandera de los Estados Unidos

Hay tres colores en la bandera de los Estados Unidos.
La bandera es roja, blanca y azul.

Hay cincuenta estados en los Estados Unidos.
Hay cincuenta estrellas en la bandera de los Estados Unidos.
Hay una estrella por cada estado.

Hay trece franjas en la bandera de los Estados Unidos.
Las franjas son rojas y blancas.
Hay siete franjas rojas y seis franjas blancas.
Hay una franja para cada uno de los primeros trece
     estados de los Estados Unidos.
Los trece primeros estados se llamaban colonias.

Capítulo 5

Página 54   Ramas del Gobierno

El gobierno de los Estados Unidos tiene tres partes.
Estas partes se llaman las tres ramas del gobierno.

Los nombres de las tres ramas del gobierno son:
    la rama legislativa,
    la rama ejecutiva,
    la rama judicial.

Los Senadores y representantes trabajan en la rama
    legislativa.
El Presidente y Vice Presidente trabajan en la rama
    ejecutiva.
La Suprema Corte de Justicia trabaja en la rama judicial.

Página 56   Haciendo, Ejecutando y Explicando las Leyes de los Estados Unidos

La rama legislativa del gobierno se llama el Congreso.
Los Senadores y representantes están en el Congreso.
Ellos hacen las leyes de los Estados Unidos.
Ellos trabajan en el Capitolio.
El Capitolio está en Washington, D.C.

El Presidente y Vice Presidente trabajan en la rama
    ejecutiva.
Ellos ejecutan las leyes de los Estados Unidos.
El Presidente vive y trabaja en la Casa Blanca.
La Casa Blanca está en Washington, D.C.

La Corte Suprema de Justicia es la rama judicial.
Ellos explican las leyes de los Estados Unidos.
Ellos trabajan en la Corte Suprema.
La Corte Suprema está en Washington, D.C.

Capítulo 6

Página 64   El Congreso de los Estados Unidos

El Congreso de los Estados Unidos es la rama legislativa del
    gobierno.
La rama legislativa hace las leyes de los Estados Unidos.
El Congreso tiene dos partes: El Senado y la Camara de
    Representantes.

Los Senadores trabajan en el Senado.
Hay cien Senadores.
Hay dos Senadores de cada estado.
El período de un Senador es de seis años.

Los Representantes trabajan en la Camara de
    Representantes.
Los Representantes también se les llama congresistas.
Hay 435 Representantes.
Hay diferente número de representantes por cada estado.
Los estados con muchas personas tienen más
    representantes.
Los estados con menos personas tienen menos
    representantes.
El período de un representante es de dos años.

Página 67   El Presidente de los Estados Unidos

El Presidente de los Estados Unidos está a la cabeza de
    la rama ejecutiva del gobierno.
La rama ejecutiva ejecutar las leyes de los Estados Unidos.
El Presidente es el jefe ejecutivo.
El Presidente es el comandante en jefe de las fuerzas armadas.

El Presidente vive y trabaja en la Casa Blanca.
El período del Presidente es de cuatro años.
El pueblo estadounidense elige un Presidente cada cuatro años.
El presidente puede servir por dos períodos.

El Vice Presidente trabaja con el Presidente.
El pueblo estadounidense elige al Presidente y al Vice
    Presidente al mismo tiempo.
Si el Presidente muere, el Vice Presidente es el nuevo
    Presidente.

El nombre del Presidente de los Estados Unidos es
_____.
El nombre del Vice Presidente es _____.

Página 69   La Corte Suprema

La Corte Suprema y otras cortes federales son la rama judicial
    del gobierno.
La rama judicial explica las leyes de los Estados Unidos.
La Corte Suprema es la corte más alta en los Estados Unidos.

Hay nueve jueces en la Corte Suprema.
Se les llama también Jueces de la Corte Suprema.
Su período es de por vida.
El pueblo estadounidense no elige a los jueces de la Corte
    Suprema.
El Presidente los designa y el Senado los aprueba.

A la cabeza de la Corte Suprema está el Jefe de Justicia de los
    Estados Unidos.
El nombre del Jefe de Justicia de los Estados Unidos es

_____.

Capítulo 7

Página 76   Una Forma Representativa de Gobierno

Los Estados Unidos no es una dictadura.
No tiene un dictador.
Los Estados Unidos no es una monarquía.
No tiene rey ni reina.

Los Estados Unidos es una república.
Tiene una forma democrática de gobierno.
Tiene una forma representativa de gobierno.

El pueblo estadounidense elige a los representantes.
Ellos eligen al Presidente, Vice Presidente, Senadores,
    y Congresistas.
Estos oficiales trabajan en el gobierno de los Estados Unidos.
Ellos sirven al pueblo estadounidense.

Página 78   Gobierno Estatal y Local

Hay tres niveles de gobierno en los Estados Unidos: federal,
    estatal y local.

El gobierno federal tiene tres ramas.
La mayoría de los gobiernos estatales también tienen tres ramas.

La legislatura estatal hace las leyes del estado.
Las cortes estatales explican las leyes del estado.
El gobernador está a la cabeza del gobierno del estado.
El gobernador ejecuta las leyes del estado.
El nombre de nuestro estado es _____.
El nombre de nuestro gobernador es _____.

Hay muchos tipos de gobierno local.
Hay ciudades, pueblos y condados.
En algunas ciudades y pueblos el alcalde está a la cabeza
   del gobierno local.
Otras ciudades y pueblos tienen un administrador urbano.
El nombre de nuestra ciudad/pueblo es
_____.

El nombre de nuestro alcalde/administrador urbano es
_____.

El nombre de nuestro condado es
_____.

Página 82   La Constitución

La Constitución es la ley más alta de los Estados Unidos.
Se le llama "la suprema ley del pueblo."

La Constitución da las reglas para las tres ramas del
   gobierno.
Dice lo que cada rama puede y no puede hacer.
Le dice al Senado y a la Camara de Representantes como
   hacer las leyes.
Les dice al Presidente y al Vice Presidente como ejecutar
   las leyes.
Ayuda a la Corte Suprema y a otras cortes explicar las
   leyes.
La Constitución también dice que los estados pueden
   hacer sus propias leyes.

Página 83   Estatuto de Derechos

El pueblo de los Estados Unidos puede cambiar la
   Constitución.
Cambios en la Constitución se llaman enmiendas.
Hay 26 enmiendas a la Constitución.

Las primeras diez enmiendas se llaman Estatuto de
   Derechos.
El Estatuto de Derechos da derechos y libertades a todo el
   pueblo de los Estados Unidos.

La primera enmienda da a los estadounidenses muchos
   derechos importantes.
Garantiza la libertad de expresión.
(Los estadounidenses pueden decir lo que quieran.)
Garantiza la libertad de prensa.
(Los estadounidenses pueden escribir lo que quieran.)
Garantiza la libertad de religión.
(Los estadounidenses pueden ejercer la religión que
   quieran.)
Garantiza la libertad de reunión.
(Los estadounidenses pueden reunirse como quieran.)